Young Folks' New York

YOUNG FOLKS'

BY SUZANNE SZASZ
AND SUSAN LYMAN

REVISED EDITION

CROWN PUBLISHERS, INC.
NEW YORK

NEW YORK

CONTENTS

AUTHOR'S FOREWORD

Cities are considered by many people to be places for grown-ups but not for young folks. New York City in particular, they feel, is a center of business and confusion, and not a place with home ties and family interests.

Yet New York's population includes about a million and a half boys and girls of school age. New York is as much a part of their lives as it is of their parents'. The city also holds out a welcoming hand to all the young people among the eleven million visitors who throng here annually.

What is this young folks' New York? It's much too large to be described in any one book. We've been able to give you only a sampling of its tremendous variety: one fiesta out of dozens, a handful of the museums, one concert, one major sports event. We might even have omitted your favorite place. I hope, however, that we have set you thinking or, better yet, set you going. There is so much to see and do here! And it takes time. As Suzanne Szasz mentioned, she, the children, and I worked for a whole year to get these pictures. Now we present them to you with the hope that you will have as much enjoyment in doing these different things as we have had in putting this book together for you.

POSTSCRIPT TO THE REVISED EDITION

Several years have passed since *Young Folks' New York* first came out, and in preparing this revised edition we made an interesting discovery. New York really isn't a constantly changing city. New York sights include time-honored places that your grandparents—even your great-grandparents—visited when they were young. Only one spot in our first edition (Freedomland) has disappeared. Some new places have come into being, such as Lincoln Center, the Children's Zoo in Central Park, and the Space Display in Flushing. For these new pictures we had the help of Betsy, Tommy, and Johnny J., who quickly learned to forget the camera and enjoy the variety of adventures that awaited them—and that await you— in New York City.

SUSAN E. LYMAN

PHOTOGRAPHER'S FOREWORD

When this book was started, luckily I didn't know how many interesting things children could do in New York. As we went along and discovery followed discovery, I forgot about the work and simply looked forward to each new trip with as much anticipation and pleasure as the children.

Since I have known Howard, Chrissie, and Pegge P. practically all their lives, I was sure that they had the most important qualification to make them the proper subjects of this book: they enjoy life, every new experience, every new sight.

They and their friends Jamie P., and Tommy, Betsy, and Johnny J., had a wonderful time, and small wonder: not once did we drag them someplace to "have their picture taken." If we went to the rodeo, we stuck with them to the last cowboy, even though we knew that after the first fifteen minutes we had the one picture we needed for the book. The children were never told *what* to do—except to look at everything, play with everything. We never went where other children are not allowed, nor did I carry "professional" equipment.

I used Kodak Plus X film outdoors, developed in Ethol Accufine, rated at ASA 200. Even indoors, rather than use flash, I relied on fast film and powerful developers: Kodak Tri-X, rated between ASA 800 and 2000, developed in Accufine. My cameras: a Rolleiflex, a Nikon SP with wide-angle lenses, and a Minolta single-lens reflex with telephoto lenses.

In the Planetarium, outer space conditions are so successfully simulated that I had to go outside to set my camera; but both photographer and models held still for a long exposure (no tripod, either . . .).

These, however, were not the most difficult pictures for me. It was the boat ride around New York that I'll never forget: you see, I get seasick *everywhere*. . . . As for the children, I am sure that it took them a while to get over the disappointment caused by the fact that they could have only *one* doll from the United Nations Gift Shop; they wanted them all. . . . Now I can write a testimonial about the food sold around New York: not once did the children get sick, even when they combined popcorn, hot dogs, and root beer with ice cream *and* Greek cookies. . . .

I took about 3,000 photographs for this book during the time we worked on it; I don't know how we ever managed to cut them down to the 174 used!

Susan Lyman evolved the sequence of the book and I made the layouts; that was great fun, too.

SUZANNE SZASZ

INTRODUCING NEW YORK

The tallest building in the world! The Empire State Building, located in the middle of New York City at Fifth Avenue and 34th Street, rises up 102 stories. It is 1,472 feet to the tip of its television sending tower, which is used by New York's seven TV stations. Sixteen thousand people work in the building, served by 76 elevators.

To get to the top, you ride in three elevators. The first takes you to the 80th floor, the next to the observatory on the 86th floor, and the third to the 102nd-floor observatory.

What a view! No wonder the building has a million visitors a year. It doesn't seem possible that you are still attached to the city. You seem to be in another world as you watch the moving pageant far below. At night the colored neon signs and the long lines of street lights make it a breath-taking sight.

Look through this telescope . . . and that one . . . and the one beyond. On a clear day you can see forty miles away. There's the sweep of the harbor with Staten Island to the south and the Atlantic Ocean beyond. New Jersey is to the west; the Bronx and Westchester are to the north, Brooklyn and Queens to the east. Follow the line of the Hudson River; trace the East River and the Harlem. Manhattan really is an island. What a marvelous way to learn geography!

VIEW FROM THE EMPIRE STATE BUILDING

Looking across the East River to Queens from the towering Empire State Building.

Around Manhattan Island by sightseeing boat is a 35-mile trip. The boat backs out into the Hudson and heads south toward the harbor, the guide providing a continuous stream of information.

There on the New Jersey waterfront is the largest clock in the world. This odd-looking place is New York's heliport, and there's a ventilating shaft for the Holland Tunnel. Buildings tower high, piers thrust out toward you, cars speed along the elevated highways that edge the island.

New Yorkers marvel at the new view of their city; tourists enjoy such comfortable sightseeing; everybody takes pictures.

The famous Manhattan skyline at the lower tip of the island is a familiar sight. At the same time it is constantly changing because new buildings are going up continually. As the boat heads into the East River the steelwork of the 60-story Chase-Manhattan Bank is clearly seen. This building, completed in 1962, added a skyscraper of a different shape to the growing group. The dark building near the waterfront topped with a cross is the Seamen's Church Institute, and the white building on the right with the tall chimney is the U.S. Assay Office.

MANHATTAN BY BOAT

The boat passes under many bridges. The first one is the Brooklyn Bridge, oldest of the East River bridges. Designed by John A. Roebling, it was completed in 1883 and is a famous New York landmark.

Beyond the bridge is the Alfred E. Smith housing project, one of the many in New York. All along the waterfront are new developments and apartments, and an elevated expressway for automobiles.

The boat continues on up the East River, passing tugs and barges. The crews are always ready to return a friendly wave. At mid-Manhattan, the Chrysler Building, second tallest in the city, rises high in the background. Near the river's edge is the United Nations' 39-story Secretariat Building with the long Conference Building in front.

Some of the bridges across the Harlem River are so low that they have to swing open to let the boat through. The shoreline has changed. The buildings are no longer tall and there are some patches of green. Inwood Park is here and, opposite it, Riverdale. As the boat turns into the Hudson again, the rugged cliffs of the Palisades loom up on the far side of the river. The boat moves south past Riverside Drive with its rows of apartment houses. As a grand finale, maybe a transatlantic steamer will sail by before the sightseeing boat puts into her pier at the end of the three-hour trip.

THE STATUE OF LIBERTY

The Statue of Liberty was given by France to the United States as a symbol of international friendship. The French people raised the money for the statue, the Americans for the pedestal.

The statue couldn't have been erected in a better spot. Placing it in New York Harbor has ensured that it is seen by the millions seeking freedom in the new world. People understand the statue's message of liberty even though they cannot see the writing on the tablet Liberty holds. "July 4, 1776," it says.

The statue was designed by Frederic Auguste Bartholdi and made in France. Constructed of copper plates, it could be taken apart and sent over here by ship. It was dedicated in 1886. The green color is the result of the weathering of the copper. The pedestal is granite and rises from a star-shaped base which is old Fort Wood, one of the city's early defenses.

The statue, open every day in the year, is reached by boats which go from the Battery to Liberty (formerly Bedloe's) Island.

Only when you get close do you realize the statue's great size. It is 151 feet from the foot to the torch (about the same height as the pedestal). Liberty's head is over 17 feet high, and the distance across one eye is 2 feet, 6 inches.

Take the elevator, or walk to the top of the pedestal, where there is an observation platform. A long flight of winding stairs lead to the head, where windows are located under the spiked crown. Unfortunately, no one is allowed up in the arm any more.

Looking for the Indians' hidden rock shelter in Inwood Park.

GLIMPSES INTO HISTORY

It's over 350 years since Indians inhabited the island of Manhattan; but, looking at the city today, it is hard to believe that Indians could ever have lived here.

At the Museum of the City of New York, Fifth Avenue and 103rd Street, there is a miniature group entitled "Indian Community at Inwood, 1600." This shows the home life of the local tribes (who were often referred to as Manhattan Indians). They lived in round bark lodges but also used rock caves as temporary shelters.

You can still see those caves in Inwood Park, at the upper end of Manhattan. Luckily the wooded area was preserved as a park and not covered with apartment houses. Walk along the path at the foot of the hillside and look up the trail toward the outcropping of rock. You'll spot the caves without much trouble; they are halfway up the slope. After that, whether or not you become a Manhattan Indian depends on your imagination. If you are feeling practical, hunt for arrowheads. There is always hope you may find one.

(*Above*) The Eskimos of Alaska. (*Below left*) Iroquois Masks. (*Below right*) How wampum is made.

MUSEUM OF
THE AMERICAN INDIAN

At the Museum of the American Indian, Heye Foundation, Broadway and 156th Street, there are exhibits about Indians in all parts of the country. Weapons, clothing, household utensils, and ceremonial objects are on display. Some of the things, such as the wampum belts, are old and historically valuable. Others are modern, such as the Iroquois crooked face mask that is used today in ceremonies in upstate New York. Many Indians living on reservations still keep up some of the old rituals.

The local Indians made the best wampum in the country and a display has been put together showing how wampum beads were made from a shell.

Among the exhibits of the Southwestern tribes are several objects from the Winnebagos and a Kiowa feathered bonnet. By the way, none of the Eastern tribes wore this kind of headdress.

A special exhibit features the Eskimos of our forty-ninth state, Alaska. The mask in the center of the display represents the Spirit of Cold Weather.

Another good place to find out more about Indian life is at The American Museum of Natural History, Central Park West and 79th Street. Among their displays is a life-sized group of Indians greeting Peter Stuyvesant in front of Fort Amsterdam.

Kiowa bonnet.

Winnebago objects.

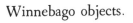

It means a lot to be able to handle things—and so often museum signs warn "Please Do Not Touch." At the Museum of the City of New York there's a special display in a "Please Touch" room. Although this is usually open only to school classes, several times during the year the general public is invited.

Here's the place to find out about Dutch home life in New Amsterdam: investigate the foot warmer, work the churn, rock the cradle, feel the dress that the little Dutch mannequin is wearing, walk in wooden shoes, see if a lace cap is becoming, and, best of all, write with a quill pen.

CITY OF NEW YORK

The "Please Touch" Room is full of things that a Dutch family would have had in their home here in New Amsterdam. The town was started by the Dutch in 1625 as a trading center. They wanted to buy furs from the Indians, beaver skins particularly. These were shipped to Holland to be made into hats. The Dutch, under the West India Company, ruled the town until 1664 when it was captured by the English and named New York.

At the Museum of the City of New York, you can climb up on make-believe walls of the Fort and see the town of New Amsterdam all around you. In 1660 it reached Wall Street, where, at that time, a wall stretched across Manhattan island to protect it from the Indians.

The Dutch were attracted here partly because of the harbor. This harbor has helped New York become one of the great seaports of the world. The deck of a ferryboat makes an excellent place to watch ships come and go. Besides the ferries crossing back and forth on their never-ending trips, there are sightseeing boats, cabin cruisers, speedboats, a string of barges, tugs, lighters, freighters, and big passenger liners.

By ferryboat to
Staten Island.

STATEN ISLAND

Instead of living in one of the early towns such as New Amsterdam, Brooklyn, or Flushing, some settlers started farms. A few farmhouses, tucked away in odd corners, have managed to survive.

One of the old Staten Island houses offers a good idea of what life was like here then. This house is located on Richmond Road and is open to the public.

The earliest part was built by the Billeaus in 1680. Later, other families added on to the original house, and it is known by the names of all three owners: the Billeau-Stillwell-Perine house.

This oldest stone part has one room on the ground floor and one above, reached by a steep stair. The house still has the high hooded fireplace and the Dutch door cut in half.

STATEN ISLAND SCHOOLHOUSE

The boys and girls of Richmondtown on Staten Island had their lessons in this old red house with white shutters. It is the oldest elementary schoolhouse still standing in the country and was built before 1696. Known as the Voorlezer's House, it belonged to the Dutch *Voorlezer,* a man who served the community in two ways, as church worker and as teacher. Today the house, repaired and repainted, is a high spot of the Richmondtown Restoration and is open to the public.

The Voorlezer held classes in the main room of his house. Equipment was simple in those days: long, wooden benches but no desks for the pupils, an open fire for warmth, candles for light, and a bucket and dipper for a cool drink of water. There were quill pens, paper, and slates for writing; hornbooks for beginners learning their alphabet; and a few books, including the Bible, for those pupils who could read a little.

The Dutch language was spoken in this school, although by this time New York was an English colony. The Dutch kept their own customs long after the surrender to England in 1664. In addition to the English and the Dutch, people from many other nations were settling in this new country. More towns started up nearby and New York was growing. As one of England's colonies, New York began to develop as a seaport and to have close ties with the other colonies along the Atlantic Coast. This continued for over a hundred years until 1776 when the colonies declared their independence.

In that same year the British captured New York, and used it as their military headquarters throughout the Revolutionary War.

Making candles by dipping wicks in hot wax.

HISTORICAL SOCIETY

In colonial days, you did everything yourself. You made your candles by dipping thin, stringlike wicks into kettles of hot wax or tallow. You cooked over an open fire, lifting heavy logs into place and hanging iron pots on the crane. The oven was a hole in the side of the chimney. Making cloth took a long time: you grew the flax, spun it into thread on a flax wheel, then wove it on a loom into linen cloth.

The Staten Island Historical Society, Richmond-town, has all sorts of household utensils and gadgets on exhibition. These are all shown, in action, at Open House Day in the fall.

A century later the situation was very different. Everyone was buying things all ready-made at the country store, where the stock included everything from penny candy to India-rubber boots. This old-time general store has been set up in The Staten Island Historical Society.

STATEN ISLAND

HISTORICAL

SOCIETY

Flax wheel used
for spinning flax
into linen thread.

THE ROGER MORRIS—JUMEL MANSION

The trail of George Washington leads to several buildings that he visited in different parts of the city. Most important is the Roger Morris—Jumel Mansion, Edgecombe Avenue and 160th Street, which was his headquarters in the autumn of 1776 for six weeks.

After peace was declared seven years later, Washington came back to New York with his troops. Several days later he gave a farewell reception for his officers at Fraunces Tavern. This old building still stands at the corner of Pearl and Broad streets, and is now a museum and restaurant. The Long Room where the reception was held has various exhibits.

The statue of Washington on Wall Street marks the spot where he took the oath of office as first President of the United States of America in 1789. After the inaugural ceremony at Federal Hall, Washington led a procession on foot along Wall Street and up Broadway to St. Paul's Chapel for a religious service. While President, Washington continued to worship there and his square pew is marked with flags and a tablet. Washington lived in New York until August, 1790, when the capital was moved to Philadelphia.

After that, Wall Street became a business and then a financial center. By 1850 the street was lined with banks, and the Sub-Treasury Building stood on the site. In 1883, the Washington statue was erected. Today the building houses the Federal Hall Memorial Museum.

(*Above*) Mr. de Frise, former curator, Roger Morris—Jumel Mansion, explains about the bar shot that was used in cannon at the time of the Revolutionary War.

FRAUNCES TAVERN

(*Below*) Signing the visitors' book in the Long Room at Fraunces Tavern.

WALL
STREET

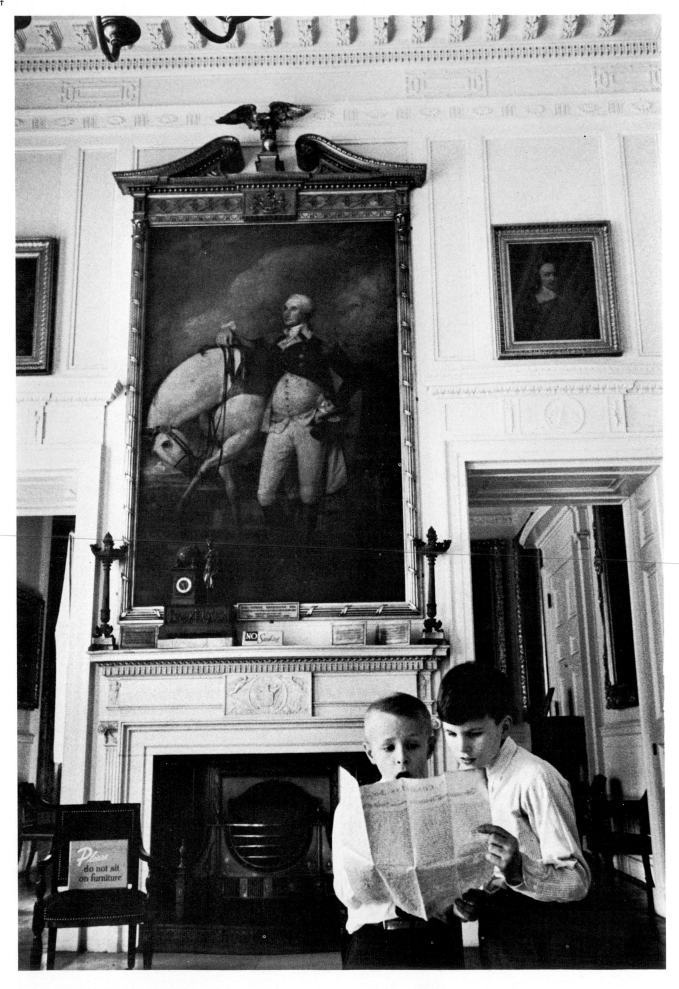

CITY HALL

Shortly after Washington became President, the city commissioned John Trumbull to paint a full-length portrait of Washington as he looked in 1783. The painting hangs in the Governors' Room in City Hall, and Washington's desk is also displayed there.

Although Washington's trail has led to City Hall, he himself was never in the building, for it was put up after his death. Opened in 1812, it has remained the center of the city's government ever since.

With New York growing and changing so rapidly, people might expect a much larger and more modern building. Yet City Hall remains one of New York's handsomest buildings and is well worth a visit.

The hanging circular staircase is particularly beautiful. In 1865, Abraham Lincoln's body lay in state at the top of these stairs. The thousands of mourning citizens who came to pay their respects moved in line up one staircase and down the other.

Under Washington's portrait is an appropriate place to study a copy of the Constitution of the United States.

CITY HALL

Today in City Hall, the Governors' Room on the second floor is a museum. The Board of Estimate Room and the City Council Chamber are, however, used all the time for meetings of the Board and the Council. The Mayor and the Council President both have their offices in the building.

At times the usual informality that surrounds City Hall gives way to official ceremony. This used to include a ticker-tape parade up Broadway. All visitors arrive in motorcades, and are welcomed by the Mayor on the City Hall steps.

Many buildings are needed to house all the city departments and offices necessary to carry on the work of municipal government. The area north of City Hall has developed into a good-sized civic center. The Municipal Building, the Hall of Records, and the various court buildings are located here.

Farther along, on Foley Square, stands the imposing U.S. County Courthouse with its fluted columns and broad steps. Beyond it the modern architecture of the State Office Building and the Criminal Courts and Tombs Prison provides a distinct contrast.

UNITED STATES COUNTY COURTHOUSE

NATURE IN THE BIG CITY

The American Museum—Hayden Planetarium, Central Park West and 81st Street, has regular performances in the Sky Theatre. The new Zeiss projector reproduces the marvels of astronomy, showing the stars, planets, sun, and moon and their motions. The program is changed often. Recent subjects: "From Stonehenge to Palomar" and "The Realm of the Planets."

The Planetarium has a number of displays about the Space Age. They have to be changed frequently because of the rapid advances in scientific development. What was new yesterday is out of date tomorrow.

(*Left*) A display of the earth with artificial satellites in orbit.

(*Opposite, above*) "Computers in Astronomy" showed ways in which IBM electronic computers help solve problems in astronomical research.

(*Opposite, below*) How much would you weigh on Jupiter, Mars, Venus, the moon, and the sun? is an intriguing thought. Just a clue: more on Jupiter and the sun, less on the others. A man with an earth weight of 200 pounds would weigh 32 pounds on the moon.

HAYDEN

PLANETARIUM

"This is a manned, hypersonic re-entry vehicle . . . when the orbit mission is completed the pilot directs the vehicle safely back to earth." Going to the moon is fast becoming reality.

Part of the exhibit *You in the Space Age* at the Planetarium, The American Museum of Natural History.

At The American Museum of Natural History, several galleries are equipped for a guide-a-phone lecture. Hang the guide-a-phone strap around your neck, put on the headpiece, and turn the volume control knob. Now you can hear what the lecturer is saying about the pronghorns, "the only antelopes in the world with branched horns," in the Hall of North American Mammals.

Many galleries re-create the ways the animals and birds live—elephants, grizzly bears, lions, strange beasts from Africa and Asia, and birds from the Pacific. The list goes on and on.

Other halls are given over to minerals and gems, woods and trees, insects, fishes, petroleum. Various displays tell the story of primitive men and ways of life in all parts of the globe and ages of time.

The Dinosaur Halls are very popular. Bones, bones, bones! Who would think just bones could be so interesting? And all millions of years old. What jaw-breaking names: dinosaur, brontosaurus, tyrannosaurus. The skeleton pictured here is a gorgosaurus of North America.

Dropping a peanut in the elephant's trunk may be as exciting an occupation as taking a ride on the camel. A pony cart drive with Rex wearing his new chapeau is more reassuring. This is all part of the day's doings at the Bronx Zoo. And besides, there are over a thousand kinds of animals, birds, and reptiles to see.

(THE BRONX ZOO)

In spite of the Far Eastern effect of this picture, the camel ride is taking place right in New York City at the Bronx Zoo.

The Children's Zoo is one of the few places where a grown-up may enter *only* if accompanied by a child. In this special corner of the Bronx Zoo you will meet, among others, Petunia the Skunk, Patches the Llama, and Honk and Tonk the Geese. Not only may you handle these animals but you may feed them. The zoo sells little packages of food—different mixtures for different animals.

THE NEW YORK BOTANICAL GARDEN

The New York Botanical Garden is in Bronx Park, north of the zoo. The Main Conservatory is huge but some of the palm trees are so tall that they reach the ninety-foot-high roof. The queer-looking plant growing in a spiral is called just what you would think—a screw palm.

All sorts of tropical plants thrive in the warm, damp atmosphere. It feels just like a jungle and you wish for air-conditioning. Do you want to see grapefruit and lemons growing? A bunch of bananas? Spices? Coffee? A camphor tree? They are all to be found here.

THE FLOWER SHOW

"Does it smell?" is one of the first things every-one wants to know about a flower. An excellent place in the city to find out is at the International Flower Show, held annually in March at the Coliseum, Eighth Avenue and 59th Street.

Some displays feature whole gardens with trees, shrubs, flowers, grass, rocks, and perhaps a brook or a summer house. Other exhibits consist of masses of the same kind of flower. How hard it is to decide which one is the best. This is a world of lovely color and fragrance.

At the Fiesta of Our Lady of Mt. Carmel, there are countless things to buy. Booths are set up all along the curb. Look carefully before making a choice! Shall it be a plastic bird in a cage or a stuffed panda? A hat with a long feather or a bar of nougat candy? And you must get a giant balloon.

One of the nicest things about New York is the chance it offers you to join in the festivities of other peoples. Some celebrations pay tribute to a national hero or an event in a country's past. Others are religious occasions.

Among the Italian religious celebrations is the Fiesta of Our Lady of Mt. Carmel. One place this celebration is held each July is in Manhattan, in the blocks surrounding First Avenue and 115th Street and the Roman Catholic church of Our Lady of Mt. Carmel. The center of the celebration is, of course, the church itself. All through the week there are religious processions, and lines of people waiting patiently to get into the church to say their prayers and light their candles.

The festivity includes more than this. At night it becomes a carnival under arches of electric lights—with the Ferris wheel turning, the whip twisting, and the juke boxes blaring. There is real music, too; where a platform has been set up, the band plays and a soloist sings bits of Italian opera.

Are you hungry? There's plenty to eat—pizza . . . watermelon . . . ices . . . pop. Smell the Italian sausage and peppers! Hear the cries of the barkers urging you to play the games of chance! Throw balls, toss rings, pick a number and perhaps you'll win a bowl of goldfish.

CHINESE NEW YEAR

The most exciting time to visit Chinatown is during late January or early February when the Chinese New Year is being celebrated. All the buildings are gaily decorated. At certain hours "dragons" cavort through the streets, each manned by a team of two dancers. Masked figures waving fans fight or tease the dragons to the sound of weird music. The place is crowded.

Lighted firecrackers whiz by, the air is full of the smell of gunpowder, and the noise is deafening. Every Chinese boy has a pocketful of little firecrackers and a piece of burning punk. Yet none of the noise and excitement reaches beyond the Chinatown area. It is incredible that something so different is taking place in the heart of the city—but that's typical of New York.

Chinatown centers around Mott, Pell, and Doyers streets. Chinese people first settled here after the Civil War and the place has grown to be the second largest Chinese settlement in the country. San Francisco's Chinatown is bigger. When exploring Chinatown, take time to look for the many strange foods on sale. They include water chestnuts and Chinese cabbages, lotus seeds and bamboo shoots, birds' nests, dried oysters, and sharks' fins. The gift shops in Chinatown are crammed with souvenirs: flowers that open up in water, paper parasols, chopsticks, lanterns, dolls, and embroidered slippers.

What country would you like to visit? What country are you studying about at school? The chances are that New York has a store or restaurant of that nationality.

In Greenwich Village, for instance, at 177 Macdougal Street, is Fred Leighton's Mexican imports. Everything is brightly colored and gay. There are lots of knickknacks you can afford, such as little straw men on bicycles and clay piggy banks with whistles in their tails. By the time you've inspected everything, you feel as though you'd taken a trip to Mexico.

When you get tired of knives and forks, try chopsticks. If you are lucky enough to have a friend like Pong Ai Chung, take her along and she'll teach you to eat this way. At Sam Bok's, 127 West 43rd Street, the first course was Man du Kook (broth with dumplings), followed by Bi Bin Bab, and Sinsulo cooked right at the table. The menu translated this as "elves' food," and it includes beef, mushrooms, vegetables, and chestnuts. But beware of the Kim Cha, which is very, very hot with pepper. *Bon appétit!*

Some nations celebrate their national holidays by marching on Fifth Avenue. The Greeks have a parade in recognition of their Independence Day in the spring. On such an occasion, it's a good idea to go early and walk along the side streets where the parade is forming. There is often a chance to scrape up acquaintance with the marchers and to get a good look at their national dress. Some have really lovely costumes brought from the homeland long ago.

Other nationalities that have parades include the Poles, the Hungarians, the Germans, and, of course, the Irish on St. Patrick's Day.

Decorated floats are a great attraction. They often dramatize a historical event or an interesting national custom in the country's past.

PARADE

Hundreds of boys and girls are members of bands and take part in these parades, marching rain or shine, and playing loudly as they go.

For the parade, many boys wear the dress of the Evzones, the crack Greek soldiers. It seems strange to see soldiers appearing in short, full, white skirts, and shoes with pompoms on them. This was originally a Greek peasant costume. The girls wear Queen Amalia dresses with long skirts and short velvet jackets.

United Nations, N.Y., is the small area in Manhattan between 42nd and 48th streets, from First Avenue to the East River.

The United Nations buildings include the tall glass and marble Secretariat Building which houses the offices, the long, low Conference Building, and the round General Assembly Building. Visitors enter through the Assembly Building lobby.

With its tiers of balconies the lobby is an impressive sight. All day long, every day, visitors gather here, anxious to take the hour-long tour which leads behind the scenes.

Near the entrance on First Avenue, the flags of more than 123 nations flutter from the circle of staffs that line the driveway. How many do you suppose you are able to identify?

HEADQUARTERS

A visit to the United Nations attracts all ages and all kinds of people. Watch them pouring in: families, groups of college students, Scout troops, Brownie and Cub packs, grammar- and high-school classes, adult clubs, New Yorkers, out-of-towners, foreign visitors.

Some of the grown-ups hope to attend a meeting, many of which are open to the public, though the number of seats is limited.

The General Assembly meets at stated periods, and the Security Council, the Trusteeship Council, the Economic and Social Council, and certain committees have regular meetings.

Brownies and Cubs especially enjoy the ground floor of the Assembly Building, where the souvenir shops and the snack bars are located.

Here, too, you will find the special U.N. Post Office.

The United Nations is an association of nations pledged to keep the peace, to develop friendly relations, and to act as a center where nations may meet to discuss their problems and try to find the solutions.

Chitra Nargolkar, United Nations guide from India, wears her native dress while on duty.

The guided tour takes you into the Secretariat Building and the Conference Building with its beautifully decorated meeting rooms. On the way you see many representatives of other nations and hear other languages spoken. The signs are all printed in both English and French.

Although no meeting is going on, clamp on a headphone and imagine what listening would be like. What language will you have? Twist the knob: French, Russian, Spanish, Chinese or English? Skilled interpreters give instantaneous translations in all these languages so that important speeches will be understood by every listener, no matter what country he comes from.

Everybody likes to have a souvenir of the visit to the United Nations. It may be a group photograph, perhaps one taken in the lobby of the Assembly Building. Maybe it is a purchase made after long deliberation in one of the ground-floor shops: a doll in a national costume, a piece of native jewelry, or some foreign candy. How about some United Nations postage stamps for your collection? There are many special issues. There's a bookstore, too, with postcards, descriptive pamphlets about the United Nations, and books describing the customs, dress and surroundings of young people in nations all over the world.

Display relating to
World Refugee Year
which was sponsored
by the United Na-
tions to help solve the
refugee problem.

HOLIDAYS IN NEW YORK

HALLOWE'EN

ON

PARK AVENUE

Hallowe'en in the city isn't spooky—too many lights and too many people. But dressing up is just as much fun.

"Trick or Treat" is convenient in New York because it means ringing the door-bells in your own apartment house.

THE

In 1927, a new holiday custom started in New York, when the first Macy's Thanksgiving Day parade was held. Now a seventy-foot Superman floating down Broadway between the high buildings has become an accepted sight on Thanksgiving morning. The Gorgeous Gobbler, Popeye, and Donald Duck are other giant, helium-filled balloons that are old friends.

As the parade passes by, you are carried along in time. The big turkey gobbler is at the head of the line, but the climax is the float bearing Santa Claus. Christmas is only a month away!

Music, clowns, floats. Lots of high-school bands, dancing girls, famous radio and TV stars. When the parade reaches Macy's at 34th Street, each unit does a stunt. It's a big show, and a completely American program. Here's a hard decision for you. Is it more fun to come out and watch the parade or to stay at home and see the show from your own ringside seat in front of the TV screen?

MACY PARADE

ON PARK AVENUE

A most appropriate way to usher in the Christmas season is by singing carols. One place to do this is on Park Avenue at 91st Street, in front of The Brick Presbyterian Church, when the long line of Christmas trees in the middle of. Park Avenue is lighted for the first time. At this ceremony on a mid-December Sunday, after the white and yellow lights have brought the trees to their shining beauty, the people gathered in the street sing the old favorite carols.

In New York, Christmas is marked by different kinds of celebrations. The foreign sections often follow the customs of the homeland. For many, the holiday means parties, presents, and gaily decorated windows. And the streets are jammed as families drive around, looking at the lights and at the window displays in mid-Manhattan.

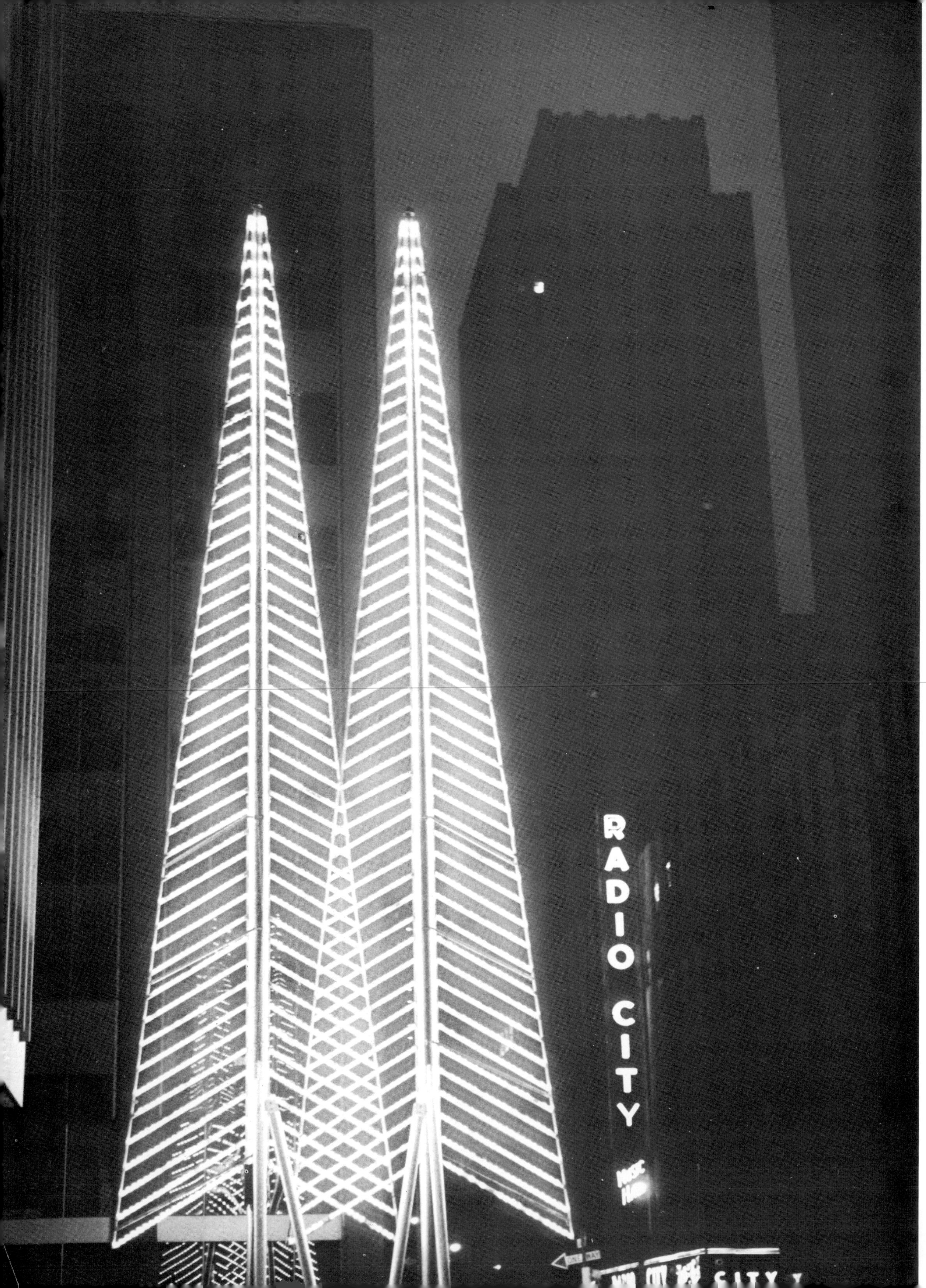
RADIO CITY

ROCKEFELLER CENTER

The Christmas displays in mid-Manhattan grow lovelier and more imaginative each year. You can see all sorts of Christmas trees, from a modern, stylized tree of lights on Sixth Avenue to the huge, real tree at Rockefeller Center. Choral groups sing before this tree; ice skaters spin on the rink below; and everywhere crowds stand and gaze in spite of the cold. And for a treat on a cold, windy day, what is nicer than a bagful of chestnuts, piping hot?

The wonder of Christmas may touch you right on Fifth Avenue among the rushing crowds of busy shoppers when you find a window display of the manger scene with delicately carved figures.

With thousands of tiny, bright lights sparkling in the night, mid-Manhattan looks just like fairyland, whether you are looking up Sixth Avenue or in Paley Park on 53rd Street, or on nearby Park Avenue.

Other windows, gay with tinsel and colored ornaments, offer gifts of every description. Giving presents at Christmas time is a widespread custom, but only in New York can you admire your gift-wrapped packages under the protection of The New York Public Library lion, who, in spite of the holiday wreath around his neck, maintains his dignified calm.

THE
NEW YORK
HILTON

FIFTH AVENUE

F. A. O. SCHWARZ
TOYSHOP

The gay carrousel in Lever Brothers window, the scenes in the windows of the big stores—the carnivals of toys, the entrancing animals doing a myriad of wonderful stunts, the bands of angels busily cooking, the Santa Clauses with sleighs full of gifts—keep you looking all day.

F. A. O. Schwarz has supplied toys, books, and sports equipment to several generations of young people. A visit to their store on Fifth Avenue gives you a chance to see all the marvelous things they have: pony carts, specially dressed dolls, and imported mechanical toys.

BRICK CHURCH CHRISTMAS FAIR

Before Christmas, Santa Claus has representatives everywhere to talk to you. This particular one was lending a sympathetic ear to a young visitor at the Brick Church Christmas Fair.

IN CENTRAL PARK

Central Park, that big green patch in the middle of Manhattan, is used by all sorts of New Yorkers, as well as by visitors, in all kinds of ways and in all seasons of the year.

The park was laid out over a hundred years ago when this part of the city was still country. The park hasn't changed a great deal since those early days. Still standing are some of the original bridges and summer houses that were there when ladies in hoopskirts and gentlemen in tall hats strolled along the paths, watching small girls roll hoops and little boys spin tops.

Most statues are for looking. Alice in Wonderland is for climbing. This is such a popular idea that Alice is hardly ever alone. The sculptor, José de Greeft, has made sure that there are the necessary "grabbing points": the bow in Alice's hair, the ruffles on her shoulders. Constant handling has made these places brighter than the dull bronze of the statue itself. Notice the White Rabbit's ears. You'd think they were tipped with gold.

Alice is surrounded by several friends. Besides the White Rabbit with watch in hand, there are the Mad Hatter, Dinah, and, in the tree behind Alice, the Cheshire Cat (head only, of course). Word of warning for a sunny summer's day: Be careful, because the metal statue gets uncomfortably hot.

CENTRAL
PARK

Central Park has several lakes and ponds. The largest lake is in the center, near 72nd Street, and is very pretty with quiet coves and rocky points. People like to hire rowboats and explore the many backwaters. Harlem Meer at 110th Street is another park lake where rowboats may be rented.

The smallest pond is the one built for model boats. It is near Fifth Avenue and the 72nd Street gate. Grown-ups as well as boys sail boats here, and some of the models are large and elaborately built. There's even a special boathouse where these models are stored at night.

When the wind falls and a small boat is becalmed far out in the pond, you may wonder if it will ever get back to shore. It always does, though you may have to wait a long time.

CENTRAL PARK PLAYGROUND

Playgrounds in the city are getting better and better. Now you don't have to settle for plain old swings and seesaws and knee-skinning pavements. Try the Central Park Playground at 67th Street and Central Park West (that is, if you are not older than fourteen). Instead of a hard surface, sand carpets the ground—this must be the largest sand pile in captivity. Kick off your shoes if you wish; lots of others do.

Busy, busy, busy. This is the place of perpetual motion, for there is so much to do. Walk along the curving wall, wade in the long "stream," capture the fort, shinny up the flagpole, clamber into the treehouses, climb up the steps of the stone pyramid—then slide down the chute. Or crawl through the tunnel into the stone igloo and go up the inside ladder. It's just like coming up a submarine turret.

Good news. More and more exciting playgrounds are continually opening up in the city.

What better place for storytelling than the statue of Hans Christian Andersen in Central Park? Here he sits, larger than life, his book open, the ugly duckling at his feet, while Miss Lydia Perera tells the children, "He was no longer a clumsy, dark gray bird, ugly and ungainly—he was himself a swan."

CENTRAL
PARK

Although the Central Park Zoo or menagerie is a small one, it is extremely popular. The seals have the center spot and always put on a good show at feeding time.

Central Park has other animals besides those in the zoo. The park offers a better chance for seeing horses than most places in town. Think of the many mounted policemen, the horseback riders, and the cabbies with open victorias and closed broughams. The horses are really kept busy.

Squirrels, pigeons, and sparrows are always hovering about, asking to be fed. When you get to any of the ponds you are pretty sure to find ducks or swans paddling around. If you have brought stale bread along, throw it out and watch the excitement as the birds snatch it up.

Feed goats on Fifth Avenue? It's true, because the Children's Zoo in Central Park at 66th Street is tucked just inside the Park Wall along Fifth Avenue. Here are the friendliest, hungriest animals imaginable. Even the frog-shaped trash basket seems hungry, for it has a sign saying "I eat anything." Go aboard Noah's Ark. (That's the skyline of Central Park West—not Mt. Ararat.) From the deck you can scatter popcorn to the ducks below. Climb to the top of the gingerbread castle, or pretend you're Jonah and walk right into the Whale's mouth.

On the way to the Zoo be sure to visit the Delacorte clock with its lovely music. On the hour and the half-hour, the bronze animals are as entertaining as the real ones.

CENTRAL PARK

Swings, slides, seesaws, and jungle gyms—wherever you are in Central Park there'll be a playground nearby with these.

Feeding the pigeons is a time-honored park custom. So is buying a balloon when you visit the Central Park Zoo.

Away we go. All ages ride bikes in Central Park, though the youngest may be on a pillion seat behind Dad. Occasionally a couple spin by on a tandem. Beginners are out with trainer-wheels (sometimes you spot a grown-up riding this way).

Up the east side, down the west side. Before you realize it, you've covered the 6½ miles of automobile roadway now closed to cars on certain days and evenings each week. What a wonderful sensation to see that broad stretch of macadam unrolling before you! Once more the Park belongs to the two-wheelers and the two-footers.

Whenever there's a good snowfall, hurry out with your sleds and make use of every slope of that automobile-free road. For "When the cars are away, the people play" holds good in winter as well as in summer.

CENTRAL PARK

In the winter, Central Park is most popular with the younger New Yorkers. Since the Wollman Rink was built, ice skating is possible all winter long. When the weather gets really cold, the lakes freeze over and then there is a good variety of places to go skating.

And when the snow falls, every hill is put to use. Sleds are everywhere. The boys who haven't sleds bring pieces of heavy cardboard and slide downhill that way. Even a few skiers appear on the broad slopes.

CARNEGIE

HALL

ENJOYING THE ARTS

Boys and girls look forward to the New York Philharmonic-Symphony's Young People's Concerts. Formerly given at famous old Carnegie Hall, as shown here, they are now held in the new Lincoln Center at Broadway and 65th Street.

Occasionally in New York you come face to face with a celebrity. But only rarely might you have the luck to be on a television program—especially with Harry Belafonte in "Reading Out Loud."

In Fort Tryon Park, at the upper end of Manhattan, stands The Cloisters, a branch of The Metropolitan Museum of Art. A trip by bus, car, or subway brings you not only to a different part of the city but into another world.

The Cloisters contains a group of medieval buildings, some from abandoned monasteries in Europe. There are chapels, refectories, chapter houses, and cloisters or open courts with covered passages along the sides. They have been assembled into a museum building with a square tower, ramparts, and a winding stone-paved road.

The old buildings were taken apart, stone by stone, in Europe, brought over to America, and re-erected. Often the building was nearly in ruins: sometimes fitting the pieces together was as complicated as working on a jigsaw puzzle. Stained-glass windows, tombs, statues, and tapestries have been assembled to bring the feeling of the Old World into the New. This feeling can be so strong that, when you step out on the ramparts overlooking the Hudson, you almost expect to see a soldier with a crossbow or a knight in armor standing there.

The Gothic Chapel, pictured here, has features dating back to the thirteenth century. The carved figure on the stone tomb in the center represents a young man, fully armed, who fought in the Holy Land.

Chapel of Peri-Nebi. The Metropolitan Museum of Art,
Gift of Edward S. Harkness, 1913.

MUSEUM OF ART

At The Metropolitan Museum of Art, Fifth Avenue at 82nd Street, you can travel back through many centuries. Step into Egyptian history. The Chapel of Peri-Nebi was constructed in the Fifth Dynasty—about 2400 B.C. It gives you an eerie feeling to squeeze through the narrow door into the offering chamber with its statue, and to see pictures painted on the walls so long ago.

By contrast, the display in the Equestrian Court, Arms and Armor Collection, seems almost recent. Here is European life only four hundred years ago. The armor is beautifully made and decorated by hand, but imagine wearing it! Fifty pounds for the knight's gear, ninety pounds for his horse's. The men look pretty funny to us dressed this way, but what would *they* think of a frogman or a spaceman?

These two exhibits are great favorites with the boys and girls who visit the Museum. After you've seen these, explore further. There are the ancient art of Greece and China, Persian rugs and European paintings, court dress of the eighteenth century, "mod" styles of today, and a whole wing given over to American rooms and their furnishings.

Shafted weapon for man and horse. The Metropolitan Museum of Art, Gift of William H. Riggs, 1913.

Backplate and hoguine. The Metropolitan Museum of Art, Gift of Bashford Dean, 1924.

Puffed sleeves. The Metropolitan Museum of Art, Harkness Fund, 1926.

Armor for man and horse. The Metropolitan Museum of Art, Fletcher Fund, 1923.

Knight's Armor. The Metropolitan Museum of Art, Bashford Dean Memorial Collection. Gift of Mrs. Bashford Dean, 1929.

Horse Armor. The Metropolitan Museum of Art, Rogers Fund, 1932.

When you pass by, look at the number of school buses parked outside the big New York museums. No wonder today's boys and girls are museum-minded. Classes descend upon a museum, spend the morning in the galleries, have lunch, buy souvenirs, and thoroughly enjoy themselves. As for the young out-of-towners, they come in great numbers, for museums are high on the list of things to see in the city.

Today's museums have exhibits tailor-made for young folks. At the Museum of the City of New York you are permitted to touch the objects on display. At the Brooklyn Children's Museum you handle live animals and look at displays arranged just for your age.

The Metropolitan Museum of Art, Fifth Avenue and 82nd Street, has a separate Junior Museum in one wing of the main building. The Junior Museum exhibits have extra touches: peepholes and sound effects, push buttons and moving displays. For example, in the popular exhibit "The Age of Discovery—By Caravan and Caravel," while it was very nice to see a lute, it was even better to be able to hear what lute music sounds like.

The Metropolitan Museum has other exhibits of particular interest to children in its regular galleries—the Egyptian Collection and the Hall of Armor are special favorites.

THE MUSEUM OF MODERN ART

Some museums give you a chance to make things yourself. The Art Center at The Museum of Modern Art, 11 West 53rd Street, has courses throughout the year for all ages. You may enroll when you are three. There are even courses your parents may take with you.

Try your hand with paint, crayon, clay, collage. When it comes to artwork and inspiration, age doesn't matter. The younger ones may move right along while a grown-up ponders, "What'll I do next?"

THE GUGGENHEIM MUSEUM

The Solomon R. Guggenheim Museum, Fifth Avenue and 88th Street, is one that you hear a lot about because the building differs so from other museums. The architect, Frank Lloyd Wright, designed a large circular interior for the art exhibits. Some people think the museum looks like a cupcake from outside. Step inside to the central open space or rotunda and look up. Instead of rooms, Mr. Wright planned one continuous gallery that spirals round and round. This makes a trip here more exciting than one to other museums. Take the elevator, which is semicircular, to the top, and walk down the slanting ramp. What a place for roller skates!

Look over the balcony at the scene below, and across at the pictures on the far wall. The museum exhibits only contemporary art, which is new and sometimes takes time to understand.

You may borrow a book from The New York Public Library, if you are a New Yorker, just as soon as you are able to sign your name. (Either writing or printing will do.) However, everybody is welcome to visit and look at the books. If you wish to bring an older person along to read aloud to you, that is all right. Nearly all the branch libraries have children's rooms. Some of them have special programs and regulations, so it is well to inquire ahead of time.

In the Central Children's Room at The New York Public Library, Fifth Avenue and 42nd Street, you will find old favorites such as Ralph Caldecott's *John Gilpin's Ride* and *Fairy Tales of the Brothers Grimm;* also new favorites such as the latest book by Dr. Seuss. On the shelves are books printed in thirty-nine languages, gathered from all over the world, many filled with pictures. Also there are encyclopedias, atlases, and reference books with all sorts of special information so useful that the room is visited a great deal by boys and girls looking up topics for school work.

The storytelling program is popular. It is divided into two parts, Picture Book Hour for the younger group, Story Hour for the older. In the Central Library, Picture Book Hour is held right in the alcove at the end of the Children's Room. Here Gail Davis is telling the Picture Book story.

NEW YORK
PUBLIC LIBRARY

"Once upon a time there was a man who lost his head . . ."

CENTER

Lincoln Center for the Performing Arts is a notable addition to the cultural life of New York City. It is located at Broadway and 65th Street, and the first building was opened in 1962. Now the area as far as 62nd Street has theatres, an opera house, a concert hall, a library, and a museum.

All sorts of people have discovered Lincoln Center. For many it is a playground, a place for entertainment. Take the guided tour, enjoy a show, have a snack, and watch the fountain play. (Hear the squeals when it suddenly shoots up.)

For others, Lincoln Center is a place for study—to learn about the performing arts. Perhaps you want to be an appreciative member of the audience. Do you know an entrechat? an aria? a reprise? a soliloquy?

No matter whether you are a student or a teacher, whether you are ten years old or fifty, you'll find your niche in the extensive Lincoln Center Student Program. Serious music students attend the Juilliard School of Music, which has its new home here. A branch of the Public Library features fascinating displays and movies, as well as records and books.

"Le Guichet," a stabile by Alexander Calder, stands outside the Library at Lincoln Center.

Seeing a performance of *The Nut-cracker* is a splendid introduction to ballet. The New York City Ballet Company dances the enchanting tale every year during the Christmas holidays at Lincoln Center.

Opposite the State Theatre is Philharmonic Hall, the home of the New York Philharmonic-Symphony Society. Concerts by the Philharmonic and other orchestras are given here. The third large building, the one with the series of arches, is the Metropolitan Opera House. Beyond it, behind the long pool, is the Vivian Beaumont Theatre, where plays are presented. Next to the theatre stands the library.

(*Above*) A visit backstage means a chance to inspect the soldiers' hats and the angels' robes with wings attached, and, if you're lucky enough, to visit the dressing room of a ballerina. . . .

(*Right*) You may want to play the Tchaikovsky *Nutcracker* music (and many other records) at the Children's Room in the library.

ALL AROUND THE TOWN

New Yorkers probably walk more than people in most other places. Automobiles aren't handy in midtown, and traffic slows up all transportation. Visitors can see more of the city sights when they walk, and they have a better chance to look at the shop windows.

"Walk" and "Don't Walk" signs at main intersections, and the white lines at crossings, are safety measures.

Please be very careful!

Good-bye, Ann! Good-bye, *Queen Mary!* This is a double farewell, as the *Queen* has been withdrawn from service. However, there are lots of other ships and, with New York situated on the harbor, there are all sorts of opportunities to visit them. One exciting time to inspect an ocean liner is on sailing day. Visitors pay a small fee to go aboard, and have a chance to see a good deal of the ship. Sometimes loading is still going on, and you can watch automobiles being swung over and into the hold.

Navy vessels from submarines to aircraft carriers come in from time to time and have visiting hours. These are published in the daily papers.

Kennedy International Airport is huge. It covers an area equal to all of Manhattan from 42nd Street to the Battery. The plain shaft of the control tower rises over the strangely shaped buildings of the different airlines. Helicopters run a shuttle service to Newark and La Guardia airports.

The giant liners load up at the company building. There' a good view from the waiting-room windows. A long corri dor leads right to the body of the plane so passengers don have to walk across the field and climb a flight of steps Meanwhile, the planes have been serviced right here, too

At the International Arrival Building, there's a long observation deck with a good view of the runways. Here, too, you can listen in as the pilots talk to the control tower.

The planes taxi to the runways at the edge of the field, where they take off. The jets are especially spectacular with their tails of smoke and powerful roar as they head into the sky.

HELICOPTER RIDE

Sightseeing by helicopter! The Heliport is on the edge of the Hudson River, at 12th Avenue and 30th Street. This is going to be very different, for helicopters aren't a bit like planes. Watch them come and go —some are banana-shaped; others are balls with framework tails. When a copter comes in, it will land right inside that small yellow ring painted on the ground. Meanwhile, sea gulls are flying all around, swooping in just as if they were making practice landings. Will they hit the bull's eye?

Here's our copter now. Climb aboard. Two people can fit into the cockpit with the pilot. Up we go in a vertical takeoff, rotors spinning overhead. The view from the glass bubble is fantastic. Gaze straight down: the lines of colored cars look like strings of beads; the giant freighters look like toy boats. . . . Goodness, have you ever been face-to-face with the Statue of Liberty before?

FIRE DEPARTMENT MUSEUM

When you want to get a close view of old-time fire engines, visit the Fire Department Museum at 104 Duane Street in downtown Manhattan. It has been installed in an old firehouse, and the brass poles are still there so you can see the quickest way to get downstairs when the alarm rings. The style in firemen's helmets hasn't changed much, but look at the difference in equipment. Think of having to use one of those steam engines to pump water, or an old-fashioned hook and ladder for rescue work. Imagine driving three galloping horses through the streets of New York. The horses learned to run right into place between the shafts when the bell sounded, so that the driver got off to a speedy start. Contrast that with today's Super Pumper System with satellite engines, and with the enormous, stairlike aerial ladders.

The subway is a quick and handy way to travel around the city, particularly if you don't have to use it during rush hours. Over one and a quarter billion people ride on New York's subways each year. The first subway was opened in 1904 and now there are three lines that spread all through the city, except for Staten Island. Very few cities have subways, so most visitors want to take at least one trip this way.

Times Square is the place where Broadway crosses Seventh Avenue above 42nd Street. It takes its name from the New York Times Building and newspaper.

The theatres began moving here from farther downtown about 1900. Then the first of the big movie palaces was built. Ever since, this area has been the theatrical center of the whole country. When the first lighted advertisements went up, it became known as The Great White Way. Even today you can see why. Flashing lights, colored signs, figures that run and jump are all around, producing eye-catching effects. From time to time the signs change; even such favorites as the giant waterfall and the Camel man puffing smoke are replaced by surprising new ideas. Look at it! One thing remains the same. The old Times Building, now the Allied Chemical Building, still has the moving band of news in electric lights encircling it.

It's such fun to eat in an Automat.

42ND STREET

PIZZA MAKER

If you've not visited a pizza shop recently, you may not recognize what is happening here. This popular Italian concoction looks like an overgrown pie. The pizza-dough base is covered with a tomato and cheese mixture plus extra fixings to taste—such as anchovies or Italian sausage, mushrooms or peppers.

The pizza man shapes a round of dough, then tosses it up into the air to get it larger and flatter. Up once, and again, and again. Then into the pan, cover with the mixture, and shove it into the oven. How about a wedge, hot and delicious?

TIMES SQUARE ARCADE

For years there were only theatres and movie houses around Times Square. Now you can go to the Flea Circus, play Fascination, poke around the peanut store, buy a hat with your name on it, or send a live turtle to a friend.

Shooting gallery . . . Bull's-eye!

Here go all the dimes and nickels. No more "penny" arcade business. What'll you do? Shoot the bear . . . hunt a coon . . . hit a moving duck? Watch your score mount on the indicator! Try the auto test . . . be a sidewalk engineer . . . make a recording . . . take your picture . . . play Pokerino.

RCA
EXHIBITION HALL

See yourself on television at the RCA Exhibition Hall, 40 West 49th Street. All of us out on the sidewalk are able to see you too because two sets have been placed back to back. There's the line of real people moving along in the background.

CHASE MANHATTAN BANK
MONEY MUSEUM

Money from all over the world is on display at the Chase Manhattan Bank Museum, Avenue of the Americas near 50th Street. Some of it looks pretty strange: stone money from Yap, soap from Mexico, silk from China, and pulverized wood from the Congo. The exhibition of paper and metal currency of the United States is a large and complete one. If you aren't already a coin collector, this probably will make you one.

Rockefeller Center is the big business and entertainment center located between Fifth Avenue and the Avenue of the Americas, from 48th to 52nd streets. The entertainment section is known as Radio City. Nearly 50,000 people work in the 19 buildings that have been erected since 1931. Guided tours show you what's happening in Rockefeller Center. One tour takes you behind the scenes to NBC's radio and television studios, another shows you the main features of the Center, including the Observation Roof on the 70th floor. And there's ice skating all winter long in the Lower Plaza.

RADIO CITY
MUSIC HALL

At Radio City Music Hall hundreds of people line up for the popular shows. With 6,200 seats, the Music Hall is the largest exclusively indoor theatre in the world. The program is divided between first-run motion pictures and elaborate shows featuring, among others, the famous Rockettes with their precision dancing.

FUN FOR EVERYONE

A puppet show takes you from the largest to the smallest in entertainment. Here in New York, more and more performances are being planned for young audiences. Some are plays with live actors; others feature marionettes and puppets. A marionette is worked by strings, a puppet fits over your hand.

Gather an audience together in front of a small stage, pull the curtains and away you go into a world of make-believe. Jack and the Beanstalk and Alice in Wonderland act out all their well-known adventures once again. Sinbad the Sailor has many exciting experiences. Some scenes produce anguish and are quite scary—then what a relief when they have a funny ending!

At a performance given by Lea and Gia Wallace, everybody lined up after the show to meet the puppet that Gia Wallace had on her hand.

MADISON SQUARE GARDEN

When the circus came to town, maybe you saw the elephants marching along the street. At any rate, you'll be able to see the performance at Madison Square Garden.

Exciting wild animal acts, high trapeze artists, tumblers, jugglers, girls in costumes, and Zacchini, who shoots his daughters out of a cannon. Best of all, the clowns! Old favorites and new jokes, they're all here. Five rings to watch at once. Get as close to the railing as you can.

The rodeo is another show that comes to Madison Square Garden. Right here in Manhattan you'll see a good Western show with calf-roping, steer-wrestling, and broncobusting. Watch the cowboy on the bronc lunge out of the chute. See the bright-shirted cowboys scramble up the fence when the steer gets too close. Hear the crack of the fantastically long bull whip. Shake the hand of Annie Oakley as she rides around the edge of the arena.

YANKEE STADIUM

All sorts of sports are played here in New York; you have a wide range to choose from. There are organized field days, such as the boys of the Collegiate School in Manhattan are having here, or pick-up games started by the boys on the block.

Many streets are closed to traffic at certain hours so they may be used as play streets. Better yet, there are dozens of parks where diamonds or tennis courts have been laid out. School yards have handball and basketball courts. Swimming pools, skating rinks, and playgrounds are located in most parts of the city. Not far away are miles of woodland trails for hiking, and then there are the long stretches of beaches in various parts of New York City.

Baseball started in New York in 1845 when the Knickerbocker Base Ball Club was founded. The club played its first match the next year with the New York Club. From then on baseball grew in popularity, whether you preferred to play it yourself or watch others play. Professional teams were organized, and three great ball parks were built: the Yankee Stadium, the Polo Grounds, and Ebbets Field. Now things have changed and teams have moved on.

New York's Yankees play at the Yankee Stadium in the Bronx, a ball park that holds 67,000 people. New York's Mets play at Shea Stadium in Queens—this park holds 55,300 spectators.

Besides baseball, New York has football, basketball, and ice hockey, all exciting games to watch—and these are only a few of the sports contests held here.

COLLEGIATE SCHOOL FIELD DAY

You can still get a taste of country (and of burned marshmallow) right in the middle of New York City. When the urge comes for a cookout, and the weather is good, make your way to the Hudson River at 179th Street where the George Washington Bridge rises high above you. A little lighthouse is tucked beneath the giant pier, on the point of land known as Jeffrey's Hook. Stone fireplaces make it easy to cook hot dogs and hamburgers. Afterward, scramble across the rocks to the river, and try to catch a fish. This is one of the few spots left where you can walk right to the water's edge.

"The largest display of modern space hardware" is the way the U.S. Space Park describes its exciting outdoor exhibit in Flushing, New York, on its World's Fair site. Here are models of such hardware as a lunar excursion module used for exploring the surface of the moon. Biggest of all is the towering Atlas launching vehicle. More displays are in the nearby Hall of Science.

(*Left*) Looking up at one of the powerful engines of Saturn V, the giant booster designed to send the Apollo crew to the moon.

(*Top right*) The exhibit in the Hall of Science called "Atomsville, U.S.A." is open only to visitors between seven and fourteen years old. Here you will see displays of the peaceful uses of the atom.

Everyone, however, may study the Telstar display and listen to the description of its role in modern communication. And have you any idea how many things a laser beam will be able to do?

TELSTAR... a communications first

AT CONEY ISLAND

Coney Island offers the double attraction of the Atlantic Ocean and a huge amusement area. People came here first for the bathing, so that a pavilion and bath houses were built in 1844. The rides and amusement parks started in the 1890's, and the boardwalk was built in 1921.

The frankfurter or hot dog has been here a very long time, introduced to Coney Island from Germany. Now it shares honors with knishes, cotton candy, corn on the cob, pizza, and popcorn. At Coney Island people really eat!

The visitors go swimming and sit on the sand, they stroll along the boardwalk and walk up and down Surf Avenue, they visit the freak shows, they ride on the merry-go-round, they play games of chance, they try all the rides. There is something in this big, noisy, exciting place for everybody.

CONEY ISLAND

The Ferris wheel and the parachute jump, two of Coney Island's spectacular rides, got their start at world's fairs. The Ferris wheel was introduced at Chicago's Columbian Exposition in 1893; the parachute jump became popular at the New York World's Fair in 1939-1940. Besides these, there are also the swooping, scary roller coasters.

Actually the rides are amazing. You wouldn't believe there could be so many ways to go up and down, round and round, right side up and upside down. From the shrieks you'd think the passengers were hating it—but back they come for more. The young folks have special amusement areas with just as many rides, but cut to their size. What will it be? A boat ride that goes round and round, or a swinging trip in a sky-fighter?

The New York Aquarium, after a long life at the Battery, moved to new quarters at Coney Island in 1957. Olaf the Walrus soon made all visitors aware of his outstanding personality. The penguins, not nearly so demonstrative, draw an audience in spite of their quiet behavior.

Inside the Aquarium, the displays range from sinister sharks to crazy-colored clown fish and brilliant blue devils which come from Far Eastern waters. Equally strange and fascinating are the tiny sea horses that, to most people's surprise, live along the Atlantic coast.

FEEDING
TIMES

12·30   4·30
7·30

YOUR OWN BACKYARD
SWIMMING POOL MAY NOT
COME EQUIPPED WITH SEALS
AND PENGUINS. BUT OURS
DO! THEY ARE LIVING HERE
TEMPORARILY, WHILE THEIR
PERMANENT SWIMMING-POOL
HOMES ARE BEING REMODELED

CONEY ISLAND

The sand and the sea which were the original attractions at Coney Island still mean most to many of the visitors. Just try to find a place on the beach, even to stand, on a hot summer Sunday. Only on a dull, midweek morning is there room to dig holes and build sand castles.

Some days the ocean is calm as calm, other times the surf is heavy and the waves break with a crack on the sand. Whichever way you prefer it, there is plenty of water and a lot of fun waiting for you. Lifeguards and lifelines are near at hand—but look out for sunburn!

INDEX